AF174072

ALLIGATOR MOUTH, TADPOLE ASS

by C. Julian Jiménez

ALLIGATOR MOUTH, TADPOLE ASS
Copyright© 2021 C. Julian Jiménez
ALL RIGHTS RESERVED

COPYRIGHT NOTICE: This Play is fully protected under the copyright laws of the United States of America and all countries covered by the International Copyright Union (including the British Commonwealth, Canada, Australia), the Berne Convention, the Pan-American Copyright Convention, and the Universal Copyright Convention, as well as all countries throughout the world with which the United States has reciprocal copyright relations. All rights, including but not limited to professional, amateur, and educational stage rights, motion picture, recitation, lecturing, public reading, radio broadcasting, television, video, YouTube, Zoom or any such Internet service or transmission, or sound recording, all other forms of mechanical or electronic reproduction, such as CD-ROM, CD-I, DVD, information storage and retrieval systems and photocopying, and the rights of translation into foreign languages, are strictly reserved. No part of this book may be reproduced, or transmitted in any form, by any means, now known or yet to be invented, without the prior written permission of TRW Plays in its capacity as publisher.

PERFORMANCE WARNING and ADVISORY: Professional, amateur, and educational groups are hereby advised that performance of this Play requires a license and is subject to payment of a royalty whether or not admission is charged. The stage performance rights throughout the world for this Play are controlled exclusively by TRW Plays. No professional, amateur, or educational performance may be given without obtaining, in advance of any and all performances, the written permission of TRW Plays and paying the requisite fee. Current royalty rates and performance information may be found at our website at www.trwplays.com and www.trwplays.co.uk. Inquiries concerning all other rights should be forwarded on to

TRW Plays
A division of Theatrical Rights Worldwide
1180 Avenue of the Americas, 6th Floor
New York, NY 10036
trwplays@theatricalrights.com

and

TRW Plays
A division of Theatrical Rights Worldwide
122-124 Regent Street
London W1B 5SA UK
trwplays@theatricalrights.co.uk

TRW Plays ATTRIBUTION: Professional, amateur, and educational licensees shall include the following notice in all programs, advertisements, and other printed material distributed or published in connection with the production of the Play:

ALLIGATOR MOUTH, TADPOLE ASS
is produced by special arrangement with TRW Plays.
www.trwplays.com
www.trwplays.co.uk

Printed in the U.S.A. / U.K.
ISBN: 978-1-63852-015-3

Alligator Mouth, Tadpole Ass was supported by a Roundtable Reading at The Lark organized by Krista William, Round-table Director.

Roundtable Cast:
Evander/Chelley	Adam Basco-Mahieddine
Hank/Mercedes	Dan Domingues

Alligator Mouth, Tadpole Ass was commissioned by Theatre Rhinoceros for their 2020/2021 Season as a live-stream production in San Francisco, CA opening on December 11, 2020. It was directed by Richard A. Mosqueda and stage managed by Rachel Mogan.

Original Cast:
Evander/Chelley	Jakob Mendoza-Reitz
Hank/Mercedes	Armando Rey

Synopsis

Alligator Mouth, Tadpole Ass is a twistedly queer memory play about a troubled man in 1986 looking for answers at Miss Chelley's Fortune Shop in NYC. There he meets a young man whose memory is triggered by their intense connection. They cruise and dance their way through the past, leading them to a dangerous evening of improper role play.

Setting

1986 / 1983 / 1969. Greenwich Village, NYC.

Cast of Characters

EVANDER ("VAN"): *(17, Male, Latine)* Charming, boyish, mischievous. A mystic in hustler clothing because... well... he's gotta eat.

HANK: *(40, Male, Latine)* Handsome, but weathered. Troubled and mysterious. Seeking answers to the un-answerable... but... he's gonna try.

CHELLEY: *(35, Female)* Mystical, eccentric, but ground-ed. Emotionally hardened because... you know... life. *(Played by EVANDER)*

MERCEDES: *(40, Male)* Evander's father. Handsome but weathered. Life has been... well... hard. *(Played by HANK)*

This play should be cast with two Latine, male-presenting actors. It is important that CHELLEY is played by the same actor playing EVANDER, and that MERCEDES is played by the same actor playing HANK. Do not cast these roles with other actors.

Key

[text] - spoken out loud, specifically as Chelley, but only heard by the audience

/ - when the next line of dialogue should be spoken

— - an interruption

Dedication

For Andrew Kramer and Sean Mahoney, whose words, wisdom, and witchery inspire me every single day.

Alligator Mouth, Tadpole Ass

New York City - Christopher Street - June, 1986

A woman turns on a neon sign in the window, that reads Miss Chelley's Fortunes. Her face is obscured.

She sits at a table, barely visible by the neon light... the only light illuminating the inside.

She shuffles Tarot Cards. She flips one over.

She kisses the card and places it in the middle of the deck.

She goes over to a glass encased candle. She lights it.

WOMAN:
Eras una madre maravillosa!

A bit of lightning outside makes the silhouette of a man hanging appear in the storefront window.

The wind makes the front door shake.

The bell chimes and lights shift.

The woman vanishes at the same time as a man walks in.

Lavish curtains and beads drape and decorate the space with opulence mixed with overt tackiness.

The Smiths' "Handsome Devil" from Hatful of Hollow plays, filling the room with Morrissey's tortured vocals.

The man, HANK, is sweating and disheveled. He waits by the door.

He is unaware that a teenage boy is watching him from behind the curtains. The boy is not hiding but shouldn't be readily noticeable by HANK or the audience. The teenage boy is about 16, maybe 17 at most.

HANK scans the room, running his finger across a velvet covered chair.

HANK:
Anybody here?

Nothing. Hank is about to leave when...

VAN:
Hi.

HANK jumps.

VAN stands in a provocative contrapposto.

VAN:
[He's got a look on his mug. It's familiar.]
Are you okay?

HANK:

Yes.

VAN:

You don't look it.

[*I know this shifting of feet. This suppressed lip twitch. It's all very familiar.*]

HANK:

I didn't see you.

VAN:

[*He has. Each and every time he walked past the window. Five times to be exact.*]

> *VAN lowers the music.*

HANK:

Is the person who...

VAN:

What?

HANK:

Does the stuff here?

VAN:

What stuff?

HANK:

Readings. The readings.

VAN:

[*He's not here for a reading.*]

I'm the only one here at the moment. Just me and my lonesome...

HANK:

I need a reading.

VAN:

I do readings.

HANK:

You?

VAN:

Yes.

HANK:

I'm looking for a professional.

VAN:

This ain't Wall Street.

HANK:

I'm serious, I need someone...

VAN:

[So do I]

It's not like all this is an exact science. You don't need no Master's degree for the spiritual arts. Either you got it or you don't. I'm very good.

HANK:

I don't doubt it. You are very...

VAN:

[Very...]

HANK:

I mean, you could be my...

VAN:

Son?

> *The wind makes the front door shake which makes the bell hanging from the door chime.*

Sure is windy out there. It's a good thing you came

in here to seek shelter.

HANK:
I have a home.

VAN:
[So did I.]
I didn't say you didn't.

HANK:
Didn't you?

VAN:
No.

HANK:
My mistake.

> HANK *swallows his saliva.*

> *(beat)*

I think I'll just...

VAN:
[Don't let him go.]
I could do a reading. I mean, I'm just learning but
I think I'm pretty good at understanding the basics.

HANK:
I need a bit more than the basics.

VAN:
I think I could surprise you. Free of charge. That is
if you ain't satisfied.

HANK:
That's very nice, but—

VAN:

I tell you, one day I'll own this place and you'll have to wait on a line to get a reading from me. It's funny that you are living on the reluctant side of this argument when I made it worth your while by offering a satisfaction guaranteed or your money back offer. That don't happen that often. Maybe never! So you should actually feel like you just won the big showcase on The Price is Right. Get your pets spayed and neutered!

>   *HANK bursts into a serious ugly cry.*

[Oh. Fuck.]
Um.... Here.

>   *VAN gives a box of tissues to HANK who takes it and blows his nose.*

>   *HANK extends his arm back to VAN to give back the box of tissues.*

Hold on to them. I have a feeling you may need them again.

HANK:

A feeling?

VAN:

Like I said, I'm good at this stuff.

>   *HANK turns to leave.*

[Stop him!]
Do you listen to them!?

>   *(pause)*

The Smiths.

HANK:

I don't...

VAN:

They make me feel better sometimes. It's the saddest music I've ever heard. It makes me happy sometimes to know that someone has it worse off than me. You know what I mean? Like I could be on the edge of a bridge, ready to jump head first, but if I listen to a little Hatful of Hollow... I'm good. You know? The Smiths album? Of course not. Totally forgot they haven't released this one in the States, yet. It's a compilation album of their hits and B-Sides. I managed to score a copy at Bleecker Street Records. The have everything. Spent three weeks worth of allowance on it. Imports are expensive.

HANK:

Sounds rare.

VAN:

It is. You've heard of them though, right? I mean you don't look that old.

HANK:

Well, thank you.

VAN:

You couldn't be more than...

HANK:

I could be / your...

VAN:

[Daddy.]

The wind makes the front door shake again.

The bell chimes.

Yeah. We covered that.

(beat)

Morrissey and Marr are doing exactly what music should be doing right now. Like so fucking depressing, but so fucking funny at the same time. Depression can be really funny when you think about it. I mean just this moment. Like you don't know me from a hole in the wall, pardon the pun, but yet you're all misty and snot. You really should give it a listen, sometime.

HANK:
I'm listening right now.

VAN:
That's not listening. That's hearing. It's totally different. That's why there are two different words for it. This is the only album I listen to when I'm sad.

HANK:
Are you sad?

VAN:
[Yes.]
Not when it's playing.
[Lies.]

HANK:
So where is...

VAN:
Miss Chelley?

HANK:

Okay.

VAN:

Out. Buying sage or some shit. She keeps telling me that I brought some negative energy or whatnot when I arrived...
[The energy of a an unwanted soul, perhaps...]
So now I carry this crystal in my pocket and always have a sun crystal burning in front of a white candle... like so...

> *VAN points to a white candle encased in glass with what appears to be a saint on the glass but the head of the saint is a magazine cut out of Morrissey glued to the candle. It looks a bit ridiculous.*

HANK:

That doesn't look like any kind of patron saint I know.

VAN:

That's Morrissey.

HANK:

Morrissey.

VAN:

He's the guy singing. He ain't officially a patron saint of anything but I would say he's saved me about a thousand and fifty times so...

HANK:

Saved you?

VAN:

Through the speaker. Ain't anyone ever do that for

you?

HANK:
I can't be saved.

VAN:
[That's familiar.]
Well, that's just because you ain't ever heard of The
Smiths before. Take a deeper listen... you'll see.

> *They listen to Morrissey's vocals.*

[He looks just like him.]
You kind of look like him, actually.

HANK:
Like the candle?

VAN:
[Like him.]

> (beat)

Here. Hold this.

> *VAN grabs a bouquet of white gladiolas from a vase and
> gives them to HANK.*

Oh My God. Totally.
[It's uncanny.]
Now, swing them around your head like you are
tortured.

HANK:
No.

VAN:
Come on... Just do it..

HANK:
No.

VAN:
For me...

> VAN *bats his eyes. There is magic in his flirtation.*

> HANK *swings the bouquet over his head... half-assed.*

> VAN *takes back the bouquet.*

That was pathetic.

> *(silence)*

HANK:
Sage and crystals, huh?

VAN:
That's Miss Chelley...

HANK:
And you are?

VAN:
A mistake.

> *The wind makes the front door shake again.*

> *The bell chimes.*

HANK:
Aren't we all?

VAN:
Not Morrissey.

HANK:

When will this Miss Chelley will be back?

VAN:

I can't say for certain, but when it comes to sage and crystals and the like, it may take a while.

HANK:

I'll come back.

VAN:

[Stop him. Don't let him go!]
That wasn't a send off. I'm totally good company. Promise. Besides, it looks like you've got nowhere to go.

HANK:

What makes you say that?

VAN:

[Cause he'd be there.]
I ain't suggesting you don't got a home if that's what you are thinking again. I just think if you do, then you probably don't want to be there. Am I right?

> (beat)

People usually come here for two reasons. Answers or fun. And not to be a dick or something but you don't seem like you're having any fun.

HANK:

Or getting any answers.

VAN:

I can help you with both.
[Can this be a do over?]

The wind makes the front door shake again.

The bell chimes.

Time stops.

You can never be too sure of a man with highs and lows. The impact of their being constantly shapes and shifts depending on their mood. Daddy was especially guilty and Mama, well... Mama just wanted a normal life. But that's the thing... Normal is relative. I think putting ketchup on corn is normal, but others would say I'm a freak. As with anything, perspective shifts and what we're left with is what is normal to us. This one reminds me of Daddy for the inconsistency and Mama for the never enough attitude. It's curious that one person can stir up so much recall in someone. Early memories... premonitions... experiences... pre-conception. Like I always was and always will be. Is that blasphemy? Again, I suppose it depends on your perception. My perception is this... Everything in darkness will surely be brought into a personal soft pink gelled spotlight for the appropriate amount of glow. That's the best hue for my skin. And the best hyperbole for everything inside me that's waiting to break free.

A bit of lightning outside

For a split second it makes a silhouette of a man hanging appear in the storefront window. If you blinked, you may have missed it.

The wind makes the front door shake again.

The bell chimes.

Time resumes.

VAN scratches the side of his torso underneath his Smiths t-shirt. As he scratches, his shirt is hiked up revealing his belly and happy trail of hair that disappears into his jeans. This is deliberate.

HANK watches. There is nothing subtle about this exchange.

HANK:
How old are you?

VAN:
How old are *you*?

HANK:
Touché.

VAN:
Oh, I don't know Spanish...

HANK:
It's not Spanish.

VAN:
Sounds Spanish.

HANK:
You look Spanish.

VAN:
Gracias.

HANK:
How old?

VAN:

Does it matter?

HANK:

It does.

VAN:

My stars, we're just talking. Although it seems that I've been doing all the talking.

HANK:

I'm talking.

VAN:

You want a cola?

HANK:

I don't drink cola.

VAN:

[Neither did Daddy.]
That's all I got.

HANK:

I didn't ask for a drink.

VAN:

I'm being hospitable. I can be very hospitable.

HANK:

I should go.

VAN:

[He doesn't want to go.]
You don't want to go.

HANK:

No?

VAN:

I don't believe you do. I get it though. I have a way of making people want to stick around. Mama called it magnetism. You ever hear of that?

>   *(beat)*

Magnetism?
[*It's shame...but go on... wax pretty for that's how men work.*]

HANK:

Yeah.

VAN:

You think I got magnetism?

>   *(silence)*

[*Hook. Line. Sinker*]
So what's your damage? I mean, you don't have to tell me or anything but I sure am a good listener.

HANK:

I'm sorry, but you're a kid.

VAN:

Don't talk down to me. Talking like Daddy. It's bad enough you look like him.

HANK:

I thought I looked like this Morrissey guy.

VAN:

Daddy looked like Morrissey.

HANK:

No wonder you like him so much.

VAN:

I like him because he writes depressing music,

unlike my Daddy who...

The wind makes the front door shake again.

The bell chimes.

HANK:

What?

VAN:

He had a lot of demons. Let's just leave it at that.

HANK:

I know a bit about that.

VAN:

You go to that place, right?

HANK:

I'm sorry?

VAN:

That leather place along the way?

HANK:

I don't.

VAN:

I seen you going inside before. You have a distinctive walk.

HANK:

My walk.

VAN:

It's all affected like some butch guy that doesn't give a fuck, but only one arm swings. The other stays at your side, like only half of you is confident. I wasn't sure it was you at first, but then just when you tried to scoot out of here earlier... well... I saw that still arm. You should hold gladiolas in your swinging hand to distract from the still one. You were a bit beefier a few months ago. Not sayin' you were fat or nothing before, bless your heart.

HANK:

You've seen me.

VAN:

Not in a stalker way. Street ain't that big and I never seen anyone walk like that before.

HANK:

I was just—

VAN:

You don't need to explain nothing to me.

HANK:

This is on my way to—

VAN:

I seen lots of dudes go in there. The postman, the pizza delivery man, the homeless guy with the white eyelashes that hangs out in front of Lilac Chocolates... I know it's one of those places. They keep the windows tinted and the lights dim but I can see figures moving around in there, for sure. Always some kind of pulsing bass coming through the walls... Bearded silhouettes swaying to that Deborah Harry... That Evelyn Champagne King.

HANK:

I don't go there.

VAN:

But I seen you—

HANK:

I DON'T GO THERE.

VAN:

[Every Tues, Thursday and Friday.]

HANK:

I wouldn't even know where to find those places.

VAN:

They don't seem too bad. I quite like Disco.
[So did Daddy.]

HANK:

I—

VAN:

Mama says it gives you cancer, is that true?

HANK:

I don't have cancer.

VAN:

Of course, because you don't go to those places.

HANK:

Right.

VAN:

I don't think it does, but I thought you might know
something I don't.

      (beat)

Did you ever go to that Crisco Disco on 15th? It's
closed now, thank heavens. I heard there was a
bartender there that had a mason jar filled with his

boyfriend's urine and lapped it up like chocolate milk.

HANK:
That's vile.

VAN:
Right? I can't imagine that's true for nothing. Someone handling the fruit goin' into your gin and T? Sure seems like a liability with all them health codes. Miss Chelley ain't even suppose to have cats up in here, but she sure does.

> *HANK's eyes begin to well up.*

> *VAN notices.*

VAN:
You ain't allergic are you?

HANK:
What?

VAN:
Cats?

HANK:
No.

VAN:
I see.

> *(beat)*

That's good. Tomahawk and Finland are pretty harmless, but they shed like the dickens, bless their hearts. I'm not used to it. I mean we had cats, but we just fed 'em. They didn't come inside.

Alligator Mouth, Tadpole Ass

HANK:
We?

VAN:
Mama and me. I'm sorry. I'm feeding you some improper piecemeal storytelling. I just got to New York City a few years back from Back Swamp, North Carolina. Yes. You heard right. Back. Swamp. Mama was going through some hard times and Mama wasn't in the best state of mind.

HANK:
And your father?

VAN:
[Father...]

The wind makes the front door shake again.

The bell chimes.

The song playing warps into a distorted memory. We are traveling backwards in time somehow. The shop becomes a wind tunnel. Anything that can bellow in the wind does.

HANK gets wisped away outside the shop.

VAN gets blown into the lavish hanging curtains.

Lights flash.

Memories circulate. Morrissey's voice is sharp but twisted.

VAN emerges from the curtains, but is dressed in a

tunic sort of thing with a head wrap. He has become
CHELLEY.

CHELLEY collapses onto the chaise lounge and sleeps.

The moment she does, the wind and flashing lights stop
abruptly.

The song cuts off and we can hear a television newscast.

It is the 1983 Pride Coverage: Eyewitness News
reporter Ed Miller reporting on the annual Gay Pride
Celebration from Midtown Manhattan.

CHELLEY wakes. She looks around, startled as if she
had the most traumatic dream.

She gets up and adjusts her clothes. She catches a
glimpse of herself on the 4th wall mirror and snarls. She
reaches for her make-up bag. She pulls out lipstick and
an eye lash curler.

She curls each eyelash, directly in front of the audience.
She then opens up the lipstick and applies... missing her
lips.

A bell chimes.

MERCEDES walks in.

He locks eyes with CHELLEY.

Neither says a word as the TV continues to play.

Alligator Mouth, Tadpole Ass

MERCEDES:

Can you turn it off?

> *CHELLEY doesn't move.*

> *MERCEDES charges over to the television.*

> *CHELLEY steps in front of him and turns off the television.*

CHELLEY:

How did you find me?

MERCEDES:

It wasn't hard. Your letters were postmarked from New York and you never could stay away from the fags.

> *(beat)*

A little mental arithmetic and here I am.

CHELLEY:

Mercedes Morales. In the flesh.

MERCEDES:

In the flesh.

> *(beat)*

You seem to be doing well.

CHELLEY:

I do?

MERCEDES:

You do.

CHELLEY:

I'm getting by.

MERCEDES:

Your own storefront? Chelley, that's—

CHELLEY:

I sleep here.

MERCEDES:

That's... economical. Must provide a surplus.

CHELLEY:

Of what?

MERCEDES:

Wealth.

CHELLEY:

Wealth is relative.

MERCEDES:

New York City rent is expensive.

CHELLEY:

The village is cheap.

MERCEDES:

So surplus.

CHELLEY:

I reinvest.

MERCEDES:

Certainly not in decor.

CHELLEY:

Why are you here?

MERCEDES:

So much for catching up.

CHELLEY:

You weren't invited.

MERCEDES:

No. I suppose I wasn't.

CHELLEY:

So...

MERCEDES:

I need a favor.

(silence)

CHELLEY:

I'm out of favors.

MERCEDES:

I'd say you owe me one.

CHELLEY:

I'd say we're even.

MERCEDES:

You'd be wrong.

(beat)

I'm curious...

CHELLEY:

There is a curiosity that lives in us all. We are curious about all sorts of things. Some tastefully represent who we are. Some don't. That's the savagery of it all.

MERCEDES:

Was it easy for you?

CHELLEY:
Nothing's been easy.

MERCEDES:
Leaving?

CHELLEY:
I wanted more.

MERCEDES:
More.

CHELLEY:
Than you were able to provide.

MERCEDES:
I worked my ass off.

CHELLEY:
Money wasn't the issue. But the static of life will throw you down like bolts of lightning. *Ouch* says your brain but the larger scar? That's in the heart. I'll pack you a little sage as it will help to heal your heart.

MERCEDES:
Nothing will heal my heart.

CHELLEY:
Now, now... We both know that's not true.

> (beat)

The heart heals fast, anyhow. Strangely enough, quicker than the mind. Trust me, I know.

MERCEDES:
I guess I deserved that.

CHELLEY:
Yes.

MERCEDES:
I need a life.

CHELLEY:
Don't we all?

MERCEDES:
You've had 13 years of relief. My turn.

CHELLEY:
Isn't that why you're here? To assure that I never have relief?

MERCEDES:
I need you to take him.

> *(silence)*

CHELLEY:
I'm sorry, that's not possible.

MERCEDES:
Why not?

CHELLEY:
Mercedes...

MERCEDES:
He needs you.

CHELLEY:
He doesn't even know about me.

> *(beat)*

Does he know about me?

MERCEDES:
No.

CHELLEY:
Exactly. I don't even know his name.

MERCEDES:
Van. Evander.

CHELLEY:
Evander.

>   *(beat)*

That's very... white.

MERCEDES:
You haven't changed.

CHELLEY:
Well, it is, Mercedes.

>   *(beat)*

Where do you live?

MERCEDES:
Does it matter?

CHELLEY:
It does.

MERCEDES:
North Carolina.

CHELLEY:
At least it's the north.

MERCEDES:
Cuidado con lo que dices. (Watch your mouth.)

CHELLEY:

No quiero hablar contigo. (I don't want to talk to you.)

MERCEDES:

You don't have a choice.

CHELLEY:

I never had a choice.

MERCEDES:

You left us.

CHELLEY:

It was an escape.

MERCEDES:

What were you escaping?

CHELLEY:

Reality.

MERCEDES:

You never even gave it a chance.

CHELLEY:

It was a ridiculous / situation.

MERCEDES:

We could have been a family.

CHELLEY:

Is that how you would have explained it to your mother?

MERCEDES:

I had to, thanks to you.

CHELLEY:

And there it is.

(silence)

I was not part of a family.

MERCEDES:

Yes you were.

CHELLEY:

I was a host.

MERCEDES:

That's not how it was.

CHELLEY:

Let's not rewrite history. You used my love for you /
to get what...

MERCEDES:

I'm forever grateful that you didn't / freak out...

CHELLEY:

I was the one who told you who you were. Are. I
was the one picking my heart off of the floor when
I saw you finally realize I wasn't your future.

MERCEDES:

I couldn't see my future. I don't have your gift.

CHELLEY:

If only it allowed me to see my own we wouldn't be
here right now.

MERCEDES:

I never meant to—

CHELLEY:

But you did... And I tried to hold on. It's my fault
too, I guess.

(silence)

Evander... Was that Hank's decision?

MERCEDES:
It was mutual.

CHELLEY:
What does Hank / think of...

MERCEDES:
Hank died.

> *(silence)*

He killed himself.

> *CHELLEY goes over to him. She pulls him in close and embraces him for dear life.*

CHELLEY:
I don't understand...

MERCEDES:
It was too much for him. He found out he...

> *(beat)*

I may be too.

> *CHELLEY breaks the embrace and takes a step back.*

CHELLEY:
I'm sorry.

MERCEDES:
Don't be. I shouldn't let you hug me anyway.

CHELLEY:
That's not / what I...

MERCEDES:
They say that's not how it works but... you can

never be too careful, right?

CHELLEY:
I meant about Hank. I'm sorry about Hank.

MERCEDES:
Chelley, please. I can't raise him this way.

CHELLEY:
You don't know for certain if—

MERCEDES:
Chelley.

CHELLEY:
Have you seen a doctor?

MERCEDES:
Chelley...

(silence)

CHELLEY:
What's he like?

MERCEDES:
You.

CHELLEY:
Shit.

The share a laugh. It breaks the tension.

MERCEDES:
You're telling me. Try disciplining a 13-year-old with the gift. He knows every move we make... Made...

(beat)

Hank said it served us right.

CHELLEY:
Mira, Mercedes, I'm not a mother...

MERCEDES:
I'm his Mama.

> *(beat)*

It's what he calls me. Mama. Hank is Daddy. Fuck... I keep talking like he's...

CHELLEY:
He still is.

MERCEDES:
You should know him.

CHELLEY:
I don't know.

MERCEDES:
You'll be the only family he may have left.

CHELLEY:
Mercedes.

MERCEDES:
You know it's true.

CHELLEY:
Have you seen a doctor?

MERCEDES:
You'll take him.

> *CHELLEY nods.*

Eres mi ángel.

CHELLEY:
What did you tell him about his birth mother—

MERCEDES:
Died.

> *(beat)*

During labor.

> *This information stings CHELLEY.*

I think it's better that he doesn't know the truth about you, don't you?

CHELLEY:
Sure.

MERCEDES:
It's not that / you aren't—

CHELLEY:
It's fine.

MERCEDES:
I just don't want him thinking this is...

CHELLEY:
What?

MERCEDES:
...

CHELLEY:
Soy una idiota creyendo que la vida no me patearía en los dientes otra vez. (I'm an idiot for thinking you wouldn't kick me in the teeth again.)

> *(beat)*

Sorry.

MERCEDES:
No... please. Get it out.

CHELLEY:
Why can't he know the truth?

MERCEDES:
Because I don't think he'd stay and the alternatives
are too much for me to deal with right now.

CHELLEY:
He *is* like me.

MERCEDES:
He is. And I love him dearly.

CHELLEY half smiles.

CHELLEY:
Who will we say I am?

MERCEDES:
I don't know.

CHELLEY:
How do we do this?

MERCEDES:
Al mal tiempo, buena cara. (Put your best face to
bad weather.)

The wind makes the front door blow open.

The door chimes.

*A gust of wind blows the actors back into a stylized
rewind.*

We hear the distant sounds of Morrissey's tortured vocals

get closer and closer until we are back where we left off with VAN and HANK resuming their previous roles.

During the wind/rewind transition, VAN's costumes reverts back to what it was before.

VAN:

Mama's bestie Miss Chelley, they met a long time ago on some psychic bitch conference. Mama was always "a mystic," for lack of a better word, but realized soon enough that the skills did not match the desire. Mama said Miss Chelley always "smelled the gift" on me when I was just a wee tot. Supposedly, I had a halo over me and that I had warm hands, so Miss Chelley took me in about three years ago so Mama could concentrate on mental wellness, which is just a blessing, ya know. Mama was never the same since...
Mama will come back for me one of these days. I'm certain of it.

     (beat)

Anyhow, Miss Chelley's been helping me hone my gift in exchange for cleaning up the cat shit and washing the windows and such.

HANK:
But your mother, she...

VAN:
Mama is not really a...
[He doesn't need to know]

HANK:
It's your mother... you only get one.

The wind makes the front door shake again.

The bell chimes.

VAN:
I get sadness.

HANK:
You do?

VAN:
We all do. I was sad for a long time. Suppose I still am on some level, but I got Morrissey.

>   *(pause)*

I have a feeling we got lots in common.

HANK:
It's a little different.

VAN:
Why? Because it's you? Ain't that some shit. Here I go and tell you all about my woes and you act like all that don't matter because your problems got to be more important. You just are completely all about yourself, ain't ya?

HANK:
That's not what I meant.

VAN:
I shouldn't be surprised. All you guys who go to those seedy places seem to be all about yourselves.

HANK:
I told you, I don't go to those places.

VAN:

Sure you don't...

HANK:

I'm not one of those... people.

VAN:

Good. Because those people...
[Daddy]
All they do is the dirty and end up...

HANK:

What?

VAN:

Well, they end up in a bad place, let's just say.

HANK:

Who told you that?

VAN:

No one. It's what I know.

HANK:

How?

VAN:

That's what I've seen right out this very window.

> *The wind makes the front door shake.*
>
> *The bell chimes.*
>
> *Thunder and lights shift.*
>
> *The album has stopped and HANK has vanished.*
>
> *VAN is alone walking towards the window. He is now 13.*

Daddy? Are you there? Why were you crying?

(beat)

Daddy?

(beat)

Dad?

Lightning! For a split second the silhouette of a man hanging appears in the storefront window again.

VAN screams and wails...

The bell chimes.

MERCEDES runs in.

Thunder and lightning! The silhouette again!

MERCEDES:
Oh God...

VAN:
Mama...

MERCEDES:
No.

VAN:
MAMA!

The wind makes the front door shake again.

The bell chimes.

HANK/MERCEDES:
NOOOOOOOOOOOOOOOOO!

Their scream straddles the past & the present.

VAN and HANK are where we left them.

HANK:
I told you I'm not like these people!

VAN:
You've mentioned repeatedly.

HANK:
You don't seem to believe me.

VAN:
I believe in the power of perception.

HANK:
What the hell does that mean?

VAN:
It means what we are convinced of isn't always the truth.

> *(silence)*

But I'll take you at your word. You aren't a homosexual.

HANK:
Thank you.

VAN:
That's good.

> *(beat)*

Wouldn't want to be taken advantage of...

VAN lifts his shirt and scratches again.

HANK swallows.

MOUNTAIN DEW!

HANK:

Come again?

VAN:

The mason jar full of urine I was telling you about earlier! It's gotta be Mountain Dew. Now I know Dew's got a fluorescent glow, but under them black lights at the at the Crisco Disco, I bet it passes as some bonafide tried and true urine. Unreal. The homosexuals sure are something. Always trying to be provocative when there's no need to be. It ain't going to make sucking on a big ding-a-ling any better.

HANK:

You're way too young to be talking this way...

VAN:

I never told you my age.

HANK:

I can guess.

VAN:

And I'm not talking any which way.

> *(beat)*

So, the Crisco Disco?

HANK:

What about it?

VAN:

Tell me everything. I'm dying to know what it's

like in there. It feels like it would be some sort of dungeony thing. Am I right?

HANK:
I wouldn't know.

VAN:
There's that perception thing again.

HANK:
You think you know something.

VAN:
I got a gift.

HANK:
Then it needs refining.

VAN:
I know about you.

>   *(silence)*

It's the reason you are still here.

HANK:
Listen, kid...

VAN:
I'm called Van. Not kid.

>   *(beat)*

Short for Evander.

HANK:
Evander.

VAN:
No, that's what it's short for, but I'm *called* Van.

HANK:

What do you want me to say?

VAN:

There's safety in these walls. It's just you and me.
[Rewrite a wrong]

HANK:

I...

VAN:

[Maybe he can be saved.]

HANK:

I'd...

VAN:

[Maybe sleep can be an option again...]

HANK:

I'd like a cola.

VAN:

[Damn it.]

> *VAN goes behind a curtain. He returns with a can of Mountain Dew.*

> *HANK looks at the Mountain Dew and then at VAN.*

It's all I got.

> *HANK opens it and gulps it down in one shot. He crushes the can in his hand.*

You gonna tell me your name?

> (beat)

A fake one will do. As long as I have something to call you.

HANK:
  Hank.

VAN:
  [Fuck]

HANK:
  What?

VAN:
  What?

HANK:
  Your face...

VAN:
  What about my face?

HANK:
  You look like you've seen a ghost.

VAN:
  [Maybe.]
  I'm fine... It's just...

  > *VAN looks flushed.*

HANK:
  Woah... You okay?

  > *HANK gets up and places one hand on VAN's shoulder
  > and another on his hip.*

  > *A moment.*

VAN:
  [Could he be... Impossible.]
  Yeah. I'm fine.

HANK:

Looked like you went somewhere.

VAN:

I'm fine.

> *(beat)*

Hank.

HANK:

Yeah.

VAN:

It's a good name. It suits you.

> *VAN's color returns. He's back to his cheeky self.*

HANK:

You think?

VAN:

Like a pro baseball player. At least the confident side that swings its arm when you walk.

HANK:

I'm not who you think I am.

VAN:

[He might be.]
None of us are.

HANK:

I don't go there.

VAN:

Where?

HANK:

That leather... place.

VAN:
And the place along the way.

HANK:
No.

VAN:
No?

HANK:
No.

VAN:
[Liar.]
My mistake.

> *(beat)*

Why are you here?

HANK:
I don't know.

VAN:
[To say goodbye?]
Tell me.

> *HANK says nothing. The sexual tension between them
> becomes increasingly thick.*

HANK:
You're not like other teenagers, are you?

VAN:
I'm not.

HANK:
Where did you get all this—

VAN:

Arm Swinging Confidence? Daddy used to say I got an alligator mouth and a

HANK:

Tadpole ass.

> *The wind makes the front door shake.*

> *The bell chimes.*

> *Time stops.*

VAN:

Daddy used to laugh at Mama for not knowing that expression. He used to tell Mama that he was the truest city folk he ever did see. Mama never understood the expression. No matter how many times Daddy would tell him "It means you're all talk and full of shit" Mama would look confused. "If you're gonna eat with an alligator-sized mouth, you better have an alligator-sized ass to shit it out. Cuz if you got a tadpole ass... you in trouble." Mama would roll his eyes and declare that he did not have an alligator mouth. Daddy would laugh and laugh. Daddy was always laughing...

Even though I'd catch him crying in private. A lot. I'd ask him what was wrong and he'd just look at me with the most vacant eyes. Void of life. Void of connection. We stare each other down in silence. He had no words of comfort. No parental wisdom. No explanation for his sadness. Perhaps that's why Morrissey resonates. He has thousands of words for despair… but Daddy? He'd just tell me I was radiant. It was flattery and a way to change the subject. To keep me at bay. Every time I sensed his despair. He'd deflect and say "You're radiant, son." An alligator mouth with a tadpole ass, if ever there was one.

The wind makes the front door shake.

The bell chimes.

Time resumes.

VAN:
You know what that means?

HANK:
I know what that means.

(silence)

Van.

VAN:
[Daddy?]

HANK:
It's been really nice chatting with you, but I need to—

VAN:
You know, you can cry here. Without judgment. Not sure how it will go over across the street.

They stare each other down in silence. It's awkward until it's not. Then it's familiar.

[Change the past]

HANK:
What?

VAN:
I didn't say anything.

HANK:
Oh.

> *(beat)*

I've overstayed my welcome.

VAN:
Let me read your cards.

> *(silence)*

HANK:
Okay.

VAN:
[Really?]

HANK:
Yes.

VAN:
You want me to—

HANK:
Read my cards.

VAN:
Alright now! Putting your money where your alligator mouth is.

> *VAN runs over to a drawer and pulls out a stack of cards wrapped in purple velvet with a rubber band around it. He brings it over to a reading table and*

undoes the rubber band. He unfolds the velvet with care and precision.

It's precious.

It's ritualistic.

It's ceremony at its finest.

VAN shuffles the cards in the fanciest of styles. This is a process. It almost looks as if he is making it up on the spot... or not. Who knows? He extends his arm and offers the deck to HANK.

Cut.

As HANK cuts the cards.

The wind makes the front door shake again.

The bell chimes.

Lights shift.

"The Night has Opened My Eyes" plays as a gust of wind blows the door open. The force blows the tarot cards throughout the shop.

Six cards get stuck to the front window.

VAN peels them off the window in a flourish.

Perhaps he levitates.

It should be something mystic, magical, and magnificent.

The Devil. You are feeling the temptation of

a certain relationship. It's hard to resist. It's addictive. Question your motives. These situations aren't generally good news. You have rather low self esteem at this time and feel that there's not much hope for the future. But, you can still change direction.

HANK:
I don't know.

VAN:
Which part? The self-esteem bit?

HANK:
Who doesn't have low self esteem?

VAN:
Me.

VAN peels the next card, "The Magician."

When The Magician appears, a new love affair is ready to blossom. All things are possible, but the result is up to you. It's all dependent on just how much you want it.

HANK swallows.

Now, let's see why that left arm doesn't move. Your fears...

VAN peels the card and reveals "The Sun."

You are afraid that things seem too good to be true. So much pleasure and joy. Just enjoy it. Sometimes we can be pleasantly surprised. If you have been unwell this is a time of rejuvenation and good health. You are afraid that things won't actually get better. But have faith! You are about to enter a pleasurable time. The Sun predicts an ending to difficulties.

HANK:

I don't think so.

VAN:

The cards don't lie.

> *VAN peels the next card, "The Star."*

The Star represents a wish come true. This is a time of good luck and fortune after a period of struggle and heartache. Good health is on its way.

HANK:

You can't possibly know that.

VAN:

But I do.

HANK:

NO! You don't. I think we should stop.

VAN:

"The Lovers."

HANK:

I don't want to hear anymore.

VAN:

You cannot stop once we've begun.

HANK:

I can. I want it to end.

VAN:

The Lovers tell you what stands in your way.

> *HANK heads for the door.*

You're suffering in silence.

HANK stops dead in his tracks.

The Lovers question if you have the courage to make the decision you really know you should make.

HANK:

I know what decision I should make.

VAN:

Yes. You have a great sense of duty, but are you happy?

HANK:

I don't know from "happy."

VAN:

A difficult decision has to be made.

HANK:

I made it before I walked through that door!

VAN:

If you approach it with courage, you will achieve emotional happiness.

HANK:

I will never be happy!!!!!

VAN:

But courage is the only way.

HANK:

No.

VAN:

Yes.

HANK:
Stop.

VAN:
One card left.

HANK:
I don't want to know.

VAN:
You don't want to know what the outcome card is?

HANK:
No!

VAN:
Too late. We've already started.

HANK:
Please.

> *VAN peels the next card. It's the "Death" card.*

VAN:
Daddy?

> *The front door slams shut, which makes the bell hanging from the door chime.*
>
> *A sudden rainstorm outside. Lightning flashes. When the lightening flashes we see an image of a man swinging from a rope outside the window of the storefront.*
>
> *The levitation stops. VAN drops to the ground.*
>
> *We are back in realism. What we just witnessed was happening in real time, although we witnessed it as a fever dream.*

HANK:

DEATH!

VAN:

Daddy... is that you?

HANK:

I don't know what kind of game / you're playing...

VAN:

It's not a bad card, Daddy.

HANK:

Why are you calling me that?

VAN:

It's not a bad card, Hank.

HANK:

My outcome is death?

VAN:

It's not the outcome.

HANK:

Let's just stop. I don't want to know.

> *HANK cries.*

> *Lightning again... with the image from the window.*

VAN:

Daddy's swinging...

HANK:

What?

VAN:

Daddy got that arm-swinging confidence.

HANK:
Stop calling me that.

VAN:
What?

HANK:
You're... calling me—

VAN:
It's okay...

> *VAN touches HANK's knee in comfort.*

It sounds like... I think there is a part of you that wants to tell me something.

> *(beat)*

It's just us. You can say it.

HANK:
I... I've...

VAN:
You've what?

HANK:
I've... I've been...

> *Lightning flashes. The image of a man hanging again for a split second.*

I've been getting... thin.

VAN:
[Thin?]

> *(beat)*

HANK:

Thin.

> *VAN understands and removes his hand from HANK's knee.*

In the face...

VAN:

[In the shoulders...]

HANK:

It wasn't until last week that I could see my collarbone for the first time. I can see my collarbone and it's fucking me up.

VAN:

[Hip bones...]

HANK:

They jet out.

VAN:

[A bag of bones.]

HANK:

A bag of bones is what I am. Who'd want to be with a bag of bones?

> *HANK stares at VAN, inviting him to make a move.*

See?

> *VAN considers his next step. He leans in and kisses HANK. It's soft and sensual.*
>
> *HANK cries deeper. He cries through the kiss and tries to break free from it. VAN grabs his face and holds it still. It is not passionate, but not ferocious. It's intimate*

and effortless.

The lights flicker. They notice and it breaks the kiss.

Who *are* you?

VAN:
[He knows.]

HANK:
I don't have a future.

VAN:
This place don't predict the future. It informs it.

HANK:
What's the difference?

VAN:
Hope.

HANK:
I don't have much of that.

VAN:
You should.

VAN holds up the "Death" card.

It's been a shitty time. Maybe the worst time of your life. But shitty rock bottoms always end up in new beginnings. You have a chance at a fresh start. But you gotta embrace it and live every day as though it was your last. Life is for living. Not for crying about the possibility of it ending.

HANK:
I—

VAN:

Yes. You're getting thin. But that don't define you.

HANK:

I could love you. You could be everything I've ever wanted, you know that? And I could be your—

VAN:

Dad.

>　*(beat)*

I can't believe I said that out loud.

HANK:

I could.

>　*(silence)*

VAN:

We could go camping.

HANK:

Teach you how to shave.

VAN:

[Teach you about the birds and the bees?]

HANK:

I could.

>　*Did he hear that? Is this happening with HANK? Or is this actually his Dad, Hank?*

VAN:

Dad?

>　*The song "Reel Around the Fountain" by The Smiths comes on.*

VAN gets up and turns up the volume.

The following might be a memory. It might actually be happening? Who is to say?

He begins to dance seductively, singing along with the song.

VAN is dancing, selectively lifting up his shirt exposing his torso, then putting his thumbs in his jeans waistband, lowering them just enough to get a glimpse of pubic hair.

Dance with me.

HANK:
What?

VAN:
Dance with me.

HANK:
I don't dance.

VAN:
That's right. You just cry. Move with me.

HANK:
That's dancing.

VAN:
Not if we don't call it that.

VAN reaches his arms out to HANK.

Or is it Dad Hank?

HANK:
People will see us.

VAN:
Yes. They will.

> *VAN wiggles his fingers out to HANK who takes his hand and stands up.*
>
> *They sway seductively to the music. It's fun, awkward, and silly... till it's not. It suddenly becomes increasingly sexy. Super sexy and intense.*
>
> *They dance with their eyes. Hands on asses... sweat running down necks... It's that type of dance. VAN continues to sing. HANK suddenly breaks away from VAN.*

HANK:
We shouldn't be doing this.

> *Is it Hank? Fuck. What is happening?*

VAN:
We ain't doing nothing.

HANK:
We are. YOU ARE.

VAN:
[He needs to be loved.]

HANK:
We shouldn't do this...

VAN:
You need to be loved.

HANK:
No.

VAN:

You do. And I could use a dad.

> *HANK puts on a southern accent.*

> *A bizarre role-playing game begins. Or is it a memory? The brain is funny like that...*

HANK:

What did I tell you about going through my things, son?

> *(pause)*

If I told you once, I shouldn't have to tell you again.

> *VAN goes along with the role-play... If that's what this is.*

VAN:

I'm sorry, Dad.

HANK:

What were you looking for?

VAN:

Nothing.

HANK:

Oh, I think you know. Say it. How many times I gotta tell you that those magazines are for grown-ups? Men. Not boys.

VAN:

I'm not a little boy anymore.

HANK:

No?

VAN:

No, Dad. Honest!

HANK:

What makes you a man?

> *(beat)*

Come on. Spit it out.

VAN:

I got some hair on my chin?

HANK:

Yeah? Where?

VAN:

Right here. See?

HANK:

Got any pubes?

> *VAN hangs his head down in shame.*

There ain't nothing to be ashamed of, Son. Not if you're a man.

> *HANK storms towards VAN, drawing the curtains on the storefront as he does.*

Show me.

> *HANK grabs VAN and unbuttons his pants just enough to reveal some pubic hair. HANK runs his fingers through it.*

Look at that. You got a forest down there. My boy is a man.

> *HANK and VAN kiss. The kiss becomes aggressive.*

Men don't go through another man's things.

VAN:

I'm sorry, Dad.

HANK:

You're no man. Not yet.

VAN:

Show me how to be a man, Dad.

> *HANK yanks VAN's pants down and throws him over his knee. He spanks VAN.*

HANK:

This will teach you not to go through my things!

> *HANK smacks VAN's ass hard.*

> *VAN grunts from the sting.*

> *The smacking continues a few times. It suddenly gets very intense.*

VAN:

But, Dad...

HANK:

Don't talk back to me, Son!

VAN:

I...

HANK:

I said no talking!

> *HANK spanks him harder.*

VAN:

Ow! Dad!

HANK:

You must be punished for what you've done.

VAN:

OW!

HANK:

What's gonna be your punishment?

VAN:

Dad!

HANK:

Huh, boy?

> *VAN pulls down his own pants.*

Wait...

> *HANK stops, stepping out of the fantasy.*

VAN:

Don't say anything.

HANK:

Van...

VAN:

Not a word.

HANK:

This is crazy—

VAN:

Not a word.

> *VAN spits in his own hand and lubes up HANK's dick.*
> *VAN guides HANK inside of him. He fucks him slow*
> *and steady.*

The wind makes the front door shake.

The bell chimes.

The music becomes distorted.

Lightning.

The image of a man hanging again.

VAN speaks as he is being penetrated. HANK cannot hear him.

This is not the past. This is not what happened. He enters me and somehow my brain interprets this as a way to right a wrong. A way to stop the inevitable. As if I become the thing Daddy was too afraid to face then maybe I can forgive him for teaching me shame and sending Mama to the loony bin. As if every thrust is a redemption. As if the exchange of fluids becomes the thing that will release the image seared into my brain. This position feels familiar. Cold and lonely... like... I've been here before but not in this body. Not in this mind. Not in this skin. Why does the coldness feel like home? The more distant the intimacy the more at home I feel. To feel the isolation through the depths of my body feels done before. I am not original but an origin? An origin of a time I cannot specifically place but know well. Who am I? From whose womb... From... the womb to Evander to who knows... Life is cyclical. A cycle that we repeat over and over again. Who am I? Who have I become? Who...Whooooooooooooooooooooo....

On the lyrics, "I dreamt about you last night, and I fell out of bed twice"

Lights shift.

VAN becomes CHELLEY.

HANK is now MERCEDES who is fucking CHELLEY.

MERCEDES cums. He catches his breath.

CHELLEY:
...

MERCEDES:
...

CHELLEY:
...

MERCEDES:
I...

CHELLEY:
...

MERCEDES:
I should go...

CHELLEY:
Of course.

CHELLEY and MERCEDES get dressed.

It's awkward and a bit comical, but also kind of sweet.

Mercedes?

MERCEDES:
Yes.

CHELLEY:
Nothing.

MERCEDES:
You sure?

> *CHELLEY nods.*

You'll let me know.

CHELLEY:
I—

MERCEDES:
...

CHELLEY:
Of course.

MERCEDES:
Thank you.

CHELLEY:
Do you think...

MERCEDES:
What's that?

CHELLEY:
Do you think I'd be a good mother?

MERCEDES:
You don't have to be.

CHELLEY:
Lo sé, pero...

MERCEDES:
I will.

CHELLEY:
...

MERCEDES:
Be the child's mother.

CHELLEY:
You're going to be called Mama?

MERCEDES:
Been thinking about it.

CHELLEY:
Very modern.

MERCEDES:
I guess.

CHELLEY:
It is different.

MERCEDES:
I know people might look at me sideways, but I'm not down with gender roles.

CHELLEY:
But this is a child?

MERCEDES:
And I will raise them to be open-minded.

CHELLEY:
Is that wise?

MERCEDES:
Things are changing. That riot that went down in The Village a couple months ago?

CHELLEY:

Hardly the sign of changing times.

MERCEDES:

You don't know that.

CHELLEY:

You aren't like them.

MERCEDES:

I am them.

> *(beat)*

Just because you love me doesn't make me any different. Besides, I've never shied away from different. Neither have you.

CHELLEY:

I don't know.

MERCEDES:

Mira, straight people are gonna...

CHELLEY:

What about us?

MERCEDES:

You're not straight. You may be heterosexual but you are definitely not straight.

CHELLEY:

Fair enough.

MERCEDES:

Straights gonna think what they want to, right?

CHELLEY:

Like your mother?

MERCEDES:
Especially my mother.

The both laugh at the thought.

CHELLEY:
What if I wanted to be his mother?

MERCEDES:
His?

CHELLEY:
Perhaps...

MERCEDES:
Are you seeing something in the cards...

CHELLEY:
No.

MERCEDES:
Why did you say "his?"

CHELLEY:
Misogyny.

> *(beat)*

Can't I be his... their mother? And you the father?

MERCEDES:
But Hank—

CHELLEY:
Hank isn't in this room. We're the ones who will have created this being.

MERCEDES:
He is in this room. He's me. He's a part of me.

CHELLEY:
I'm talking biologically.

MERCEDES:
Family isn't genetics.

CHELLEY:
Sure, but... Never mind.

MERCEDES:
Why?

CHELLEY:
Because my words are getting twisted.

MERCEDES:
You never wanted children. / You told me that.

CHELLEY:
I know.

MERCEDES:
So I don't understand. / That's why we just...

CHELLEY:
It's just not—

MERCEDES:
You told me that I should be able to have everything anyone else has. / You told me that.

CHELLEY:
And I meant it.

MERCEDES:
Okay, so...

CHELLEY:
Who will I be?

MERCEDES:

...

CHELLEY:

We are... We're supposed to be this...

MERCEDES:

Family.

CHELLEY:

Okay...

MERCEDES:

We will be... A chosen family.

CHELLEY:

Then who will I be?

MERCEDES:

I don't know. Anybody you want to be.

CHELLEY:

That's not exactly true. You've already made decisions.

MERCEDES:

I—

CHELLEY:

I need to make decisions too. I need to choose my family too!

MERCEDES:

If you don't want to do this...

CHELLEY:

It's not that.

MERCEDES:

We can / stop trying...

CHELLEY:
I want to do this. I love you.

MERCEDES:
Chelley...

CHELLEY:
Do you love me?

MERCEDES:
I absolutely do.

CHELLEY:
Then who will I be?

> *(beat)*

MERCEDES:
Our miracle.

> *(silence)*

I should go.

> *MERCEDES heads towards the door. He stops without looking back.*

Thank you, Chelley.

CHELLEY:
Don't thank me yet.

> *CHELLEY references her belly.*

Who knows what's happening in here!

MERCEDES:
A pre-emptive thank you never hurt anyone.

CHELLEY:
Firsts for everything.

MERCEDES *blows her a kiss and leaves.*

The bell chimes.

CHELLEY *watches him go.*

A moment passes.

CHELLEY *turns and feels something inside.*

Ahhhhh...

She looks down. Her belly grows, almost as it is inflating right before her very eyes. She is suddenly nine months pregnant.

Pain.

Oooooooooo....

(beat)

AHHHHHHHHHH!

CHELLEY *gets down on her knees as she holds her belly. She grunts in pain.*

"Reel Around the Fountain" by The Smiths is playing distantly... almost muffled.

CHELLEY *hears the music. She looks confused.*

Where is it coming from?

She looks down at her belly. She sits back and closes her legs and the music muffles even further.

She spreads her legs and the music gets louder. It's

coming from inside.

She starts breathing in quick short breaths (very Lamaze Method).

AHHHHH... Damn it...

Music gets louder.

She pushes.

Music gets louder.

Pushes.

Louder.

PUSHES!

LOUDER!!!

She pushes the hardest she's ever pushed.

On the last push, the music blares as if it has emerged from under water.

Lights swell.

The room has become a concert hall as CHELLEY does a forward roll, over her head and stands... giving birth to her/himself...

She emerges as VAN... umbilical cord and all.

VAN dances to the music like we left him when he was dancing with HANK.

Alligator Mouth, Tadpole Ass

He swings the umbilical cord around like Morrissey swings his microphone chord.

It's a lip sync.

It's an embodiment.

It's an homage.

As we draw near the end of the song, HANK suddenly appears. He dances with VAN.

As they dance they end up in the same sexual position they were in when we saw them last.

After a series of bountiful thrusts to the beat of the music, HANK cums inside VAN.

Lights shift.

Back to reality.

HANK:
I... I'm...

VAN:
[He's your dad.]

HANK begins to cry. He bends down, hugs VAN, and whispers in his ear.

HANK:
You're radiant, son.

HANK pulls out and buttons his pants.

They don't look at one another.

HANK runs out of the shop.

The bell chimes.

"Please, Please, Please Let Me Get What I Want" plays.

VAN gets dressed, but not in his clothes. As CHELLEY.

She lights a few candles.

She sees the "Death" card on the table. She kisses it as the last notes of Hatful of Hollow plays.

Lights down.

End of Play.